My
FUTURE
CAREER

Working in

Banking and Finance

Margaret McAlpine

GARETH**STEVENS**
GS
PUBLISHING
A WRC Media Company

Please visit our web site at: **www.garethstevens.com**
For a free color catalog describing Gareth Stevens Publishing's
list of high-quality books and multimedia programs, call
1-800-542-2595 (USA) or 1-800-387-3178 (Canada).
Gareth Stevens Publishing's fax: (414) 332-3567.

Library of Congress Cataloging-in-Publication Data

McAlpine, Margaret.
  Working in banking and finance / Margaret McAlpine.
      p. cm. — (My future career)
  Includes bibliographical references and index.
  ISBN 0-8368-4772-5 (lib. bdg.)
    1. Banks and banking—Vocational guidance—Juvenile literature.
  2. Finance—Vocational guidance—Juvenile literature. I. Title. II. Series.
  HG1609.M33   2005
  332.1'023—dc22   2005042523

This edition first published in 2006 by
Gareth Stevens Publishing
A WRC Media Company
330 West Olive Street, Suite 100
Milwaukee, Wisconsin 53212 USA

This U.S. edition copyright © 2006 by Gareth Stevens, Inc. Original
edition copyright © 2005 by Hodder Wayland. First published in 2005
by Hodder Wayland, an imprint of Hodder Children's Books.

Editor: Dorothy L. Gibbs
Inside design: Peta Morey
Cover design: Melissa Valuch

Picture Credits
Corbis: Pallava Bagla 28; Paul Barton 19 (top); Bettmann Archives 53; Gary
Buss 21; Darama 8, 15; Larry Downing/Reuters 31, 33; Robert Essel NYC 54; Najiah
Feanny 44; Jon Feingersh 27 (left), 48; Gunter Marx Photography 29; Henley &
Savage 25; Ralf-Finn Hestoft 30; Lee Jae-Won/Reuters 51 (right); JLP/Jose L. Pelaez
5, 16; Michael Keller 20, 36; Kit Kittle 32; Richard Klune 39; Robert Landau 13;
Rob Lewine 4; James Leynse 52, 57; LWA-JDC 11; Robert Maass 47; Tom & Dee
Ann McCarthy 24; O'Brien Productions 34; Gabe Palmer 43 (bottom); H. Prinz 10;
Reuters 9, 17, 35, 49, 56, 59 (bottom); Rick Rickman/NewSport 12; Chuck Savage
6; Martin H. Simon 7; Gerhard Steiner 38; William Taufic 27 (right); Wes Thompson
19 (bottom); Adam Woolfitt 37. **Corbis SABA:** Najiah Feanny 43 (top); Tom
Wagner 46. **Getty Images:** cover, Christopher Bissell/Stone 22; Robert Mort/
Stone 55; Charlotte Nation/Stone 14; Greg Pease/Stone 41; Jon Riley/Stone 45.
TopFoto: The Image Works 59 (top); Phil Wilkinson 23; Wirepix/The Image Works
40. TopFoto/UPPA 51 (left). **Note:** Photographs illustrating "A day in the life of . . ."
pages are posed by models.

Gareth Stevens Publishing thanks the following individuals and organizations
for their professional assistance: Milliman Consultants and Actuaries; Larry E.
Leskovsek, Senior Vice President and CFO, First Federal Savings Bank of Wisconsin;
Steven Crane, Associate Professor of Economics, Marquette University; Mike
Weidenbaum, President/Agent, American Advantage Insurance Group; Richard W.
Weening, President and CEO, Quaestus & Co., Inc.; and Terence Lynch, Vice
President/Investments, Smith Barney.

Printed in China

1 2 3 4 5 6 7 8 9 09 08 07 06 05

Contents

Words that appear in the text in **bold**
type are defined in the glossary.

Accountant

What is an accountant?

Accountants maintain, or manage the maintenance of, financial records for businesses, organizations, and individuals and prepare and **audit** financial reports. They make sure that clients' financial records are up-to-date, accurate, and complete. For businesses and other organizations, these records must contain the details of all financial transactions, particularly money earned (income and profits) and money spent (expenses and losses).

Accountants help their clients with a wide variety of financial matters, from preparing their tax returns to starting their own businesses.

Some accountants also assist business clients with financial decision making, giving them advice, for example, on buying new equipment, moving to new locations, or adding to staff.

Because a growing number of clients are seeking to use a single, trusted firm or individual to handle all of their financial matters, some accountants are now assisting with investments and **asset** management and are acting as personal financial advisors and budget counselors.

The First Coins

Before people used money to pay for things they needed, they **bartered** goods. Some of the first people to make and use coins lived in about 600 B.C., in Lydia, a kingdom in Asia Minor (present-day Turkey). Lydian coins were about the size of a U. S. nickel, as thick as a pebble, and made of electrum, an **alloy** of gold and silver.

Working with computer spreadsheet programs is routine for an accountant.

Accountants work either as employees of businesses and organizations or in private practice. Accountants in private practice are often called public accountants. They work independently and may be self-employed or associated with a firm of accountants. Public accounting firms range in size from small two- or three-person operations to huge multinational organizations. Many public accountants are CPAs, or Certified Public Accountants, which means that they have met strict requirements for licensing by a State Board of Accountancy.

Main responsibilities of an accountant

The accounting profession includes a number of different fields with widely varying responsibilities.

The responsibilities of public accountants can include:

- maintaining financial records and accounts
- preparing monthly, quarterly, or annual financial statements
- keeping up with financial laws and regulations and making sure clients' financial affairs are handled legally and **ethically**
- interpreting tax laws and filing tax returns
- monitoring how funds are being used
- detecting financial problems and suggesting how they can be resolved
- making sure electronic financial systems are running efficiently
- performing audits or examining records and reports prepared by other accountants

Self-employed accountants will often go to their clients' places of business and work with the financial records on-site.

Good Points and Bad Points

"My job involves a lot more than just working with numbers. I especially enjoy the legal aspects, such as giving advice to clients about what they can do with their money without breaking any laws."

"Sometimes, I have to act tough with clients to make it very clear that something they want to do is not legally possible. These kinds of discussions become especially difficult when clients argue with me."

Management accountants, or corporate accountants, work as employees of companies or organizations. Some of their main responsibilities include:

- keeping financial records
- preparing financial reports
- setting up and monitoring budgets
- managing assets and expenses
- evaluating overall financial performance
- analyzing and interpreting financial information to guide decision making
- participating in activities related to planning organizational strategies and new developments

Accountants and other financial representatives of large companies are sometimes called on to provide evidence and information in formal investigations.

Some accountants work as internal auditors for organizations, examining and evaluating financial records, management, systems, and controls to guard against wastefulness or **fraud**.

Government accountants work for federal, state, and local government offices and agencies. Their duties typically include:

- maintaining office or agency financial records
- monitoring **revenues** and **expenditures**
- examining or auditing office or agency records or the records of organizations or individuals regulated or subject to taxation by the office or agency
- making sure that all financial activities **comply** with related laws, regulations, and standards

Main qualifications of an accountant

Math skills

Most accounting tasks involve calculations and other ways of working with numbers, so accountants must be able to deal with numerical facts and figures competently, quickly, and confidently.

Knowledge of business and commerce

Whether they work for a single company or for many different clients, accountants must keep themselves up-to-date on the world of business and finance. This knowledge is essential for providing employers and clients with the best possible advice.

Interpersonal skills

Accountants and auditors have to be as good working with people as they are working with numbers. Good accountant-client relationships depend on mutual understanding and respect, which cannot develop if the accountant is cold or unfriendly.

Clients must be able to trust their accountants and depend on them to explain complex financial matters in terms that are easy to understand.

Integrity

Because clients' financial decisions are largely based on accountants' information and advice, accountants have an obligation to be honest and trustworthy and to deliver information that is accurate and complete. They also must be sure their advice is heard and understood, and if a client asks an accountant to do anything illegal or unethical, the accountant must refuse.

Communication skills

To explain complicated financial material in simple language or write clear, complete reports, accountants need to have strong communication skills.

Accountants are essential to the efficient running of a country's economy. Here, accountants in war-torn Iraq prepare payments for workers in the country's electric company.

fact file

Accounting and auditing jobs require at least a bachelor's degree in accounting, and many jobs require a master's degree, in accounting or in business administration with an accounting focus. For some jobs, accountants must be CPAs or have some other kind of professional certification. Most certificates and licenses are obtained through state boards of regulation and licensing.

Discretion

Accountants come to know a lot about clients' backgrounds and financial situations, but they must always be sure to keep private or personal information confidential.

Computer skills

Electronic databases and special accounting software have made the tasks of money management, recordkeeping, and financial reporting much faster and easier than outdated manual accounting methods. Because certain computer formats are now industry standards, all accounting professionals must be able to use the software that produces them. Many accountants and auditors now assist in the design and development of electronic financial systems and computer software programs.

Martina Ray

Martina is a trainee in the audit department of a very large accounting firm. She has been working for this firm for two years, while completing her master's degree in accounting. Her goal is to be licensed as a CPA.

9:00 a.m. As usual, I'm working away from the office. I will be spending the next couple of weeks at a client's location, assisting an accounting team with a year-end audit of that organization's financial records. I'm the only on-site auditor. My job is to review financial records and compile the information our senior accountants need to complete the audit.

I've been given my own desk and computer at the client's site and have been introduced to the staff. The accounting and bookkeeping employees seem a little frightened of me, so I'll try to be extra friendly to put them at ease.

10:00 a.m. The client is a housing association that builds and **renovates** properties to rent to families with low incomes who need a decent place to live. My first step is to familiarize myself with the organization's bookkeeping system and financial records.

Accountants have to enjoy working with numbers and be quick to spot financial irregularities and mistakes in calculations.

Checking and rechecking computerized or electronic records is an important part of the job. Accountants can never be too careful.

11:00 a.m. I spend the rest of the morning talking with the organization's director. She answers questions about the organization and gives me a list of people I will need to contact this week.

2:00 p.m. I take a short break to eat a late lunch.

2:30 p.m. I work with the bookkeeper for a couple of hours, going over some of the electronic financial records.

4:30 p.m. I call my firm to check in and report what I have accomplished today. Because I'm still a trainee, my work must be carefully monitored and reviewed.

5:00 p.m. I'm feeling exhausted. The first day of an audit is always hard work, but I'll soon feel at home here.

Actuary

What is an actuary?

Actuaries are, primarily, mathematicians who calculate economic **risks** and design insurance policies and **pension** plans that provide good protection for buyers and fair returns for insurance and **investment** companies.

Insurance policies are based on risks. Actuaries gather and analyze information to determine the probability of events such as illness, injury, death, property loss, or disability and to estimate the costs of these events.

Even animals can be insured. When expensive racehorses are injured or die, the loss of the animals and their use (to earn money winning races) can be worth millions of dollars to owners and investors.

Using sophisticated computer software, they perform complicated mathematical calculations to figure out how many people might want insurance protection

Ancient Insurance

The Code of Hammurabi, which was a set of laws drawn up in Babylonian times, about 2,100 years before the birth of Jesus Christ, included an early form of property insurance. Traders paid to guarantee the safe arrival of their goods, by **caravan** or ship, at a time when transporters had to face pirates, robbers, severe weather, injury to their animals, and damage to their vessels.

for these risks and how many are likely to make a **claim**. The secret of success for insurance companies lies in the accuracy of actuaries' calculations.

An insurance company charges people certain amounts of money, called premiums, to protect, for example, cars, homes, or other property. If insured property is damaged or destroyed, then the insurance company pays to have it repaired or replaced. Actuaries help insurers determine premiums that are competitive with other companies and, at the same time, provide enough money to cover claims and to meet the insurance companies' costs of doing business and making **profits**.

In many places, laws require that people who own automobiles be insured for losses such as property damage, personal injuries, or theft.

Main responsibilities of an actuary

Compared to most other professions, the number of actuaries is relatively few. About half of all actuaries are employed by insurance companies, where their responsibilities typically include:

- analyzing various kinds of risks and calculating the costs of possible insurance claims related to those risks
- designing and developing insurance policies, pension plans, and other products that reduce the financial impact, on people and businesses, of events that result in losses related to life, health, property, and investments
- creating probability tables showing the likelihood of events resulting in claims

Most actuaries work with large organizations or government agencies, but some also meet with policyholders directly, especially to simplify or explain complex financial products.

Good Points and Bad Points

"I have always enjoyed mathematics and statistics. As soon as I found out and was able to understand what actuaries did, I knew it was the kind of job I wanted."

"My responsibilities can be frightening. Mistakes in my calculations or solutions can cost a client a lot of money. My job can also be very demanding. There are no shortcuts in risk assessment, and I know that I must always work in a steady, methodical way."

- estimating the amount an insurance company may have to pay in claims
- making sure that premium amounts cover the costs of claims and all other company expenses
- addressing particular financial questions, such as the amount of contributions to a pension plan that would be needed to produce a particular level of retirement income

Some actuaries specialize in investments, using their mathematical, business, and economic skills to calculate financial risks and provide advice on how money should be invested.

Main qualifications of an actuary

Mathematics background
Above all, actuaries are mathematicians, so they must have a lot of knowledge and training in mathematics and must be able to work skillfully with calculus, probability, and statistics.

Business knowledge
Although working with numbers is the main focus of an actuary's job, business also plays an important role. Familiarity with accounting, finance, insurance, and economics can be particularly useful.

Some actuaries work as teachers and researchers in mathematics or actuarial science programs at colleges and universities. Along with these responsibilities, they may also do actuarial consulting on a part-time basis.

A logical, analytical mind
Being able to think through situations, step by step, is important for actuaries. Working as an actuary is not a job for someone who likes to take risks or act on intuition. This job requires a sharp mind that is prepared to sift through and analyze a lot of information and is able to make sound decisions and accurate calculations.

Problem-solving skills
A big part of an actuary's analytical responsibilities lies in using knowledge, logic, and numerical skills to solve problems. Actuaries are a lot like scientists in the way they deal with problems, defining the problems, gathering data, proposing possible solutions, and running tests to find the best solutions.

A lot of the information that goes into economic and financial reports and documents is produced by actuaries.

fact file

A college degree is an essential requirement to be an actuary. Most actuaries have a degree in mathematics, actuarial science, statistics, or some field of business. Beyond a degree, job experience becomes very important, and to gain full professional status, actuaries must pass a series of exams, in one or more actuarial specialties, conducted by two professional actuarial societies.

Computer skills

Twentieth-century technology has given actuaries the ability to work much faster and more accurately. Today's actuaries must be able to use computers and specialized programs and software confidently.

Communication skills

The work of actuaries is extremely complicated, which means they have to be prepared to explain confusing information to business executives, government officials, policyholders, and many other people, all of whom have different levels of knowledge and education. Actuaries must also be able to record information clearly in written reports.

A day in the life of an actuary

Sara James

Sara has a master's degree in mathematics and graduated with high honors. For the past five years, she has worked as an actuary for a large financial investments company.

9:00 a.m. I'm working on a new type of pension plan that allows people to contribute varying amounts at different times during their working lives and requires no payments at certain times and under certain conditions. Today, I'm gathering data to help me determine how many people already paying into pensions might be interested in a more flexible plan.

9:30 a.m. To figure out possible ways to calculate numbers of future customers, I have to analyze the ways people have spent money in the past and compare these findings to the way people live today. A task like this is difficult, but without my computer, it would take years!

12:00 p.m. During lunch, I start preparing my notes for a progress meeting this afternoon. I have to update my colleagues on the work I've completed for designing the new pension plan.

2:00 p.m. At the progress meeting, people from various departments report on the development of several new plans for insurance policies and **annuities**. Our marketing department thinks these policies will be very successful and is impatient to get them into the marketplace. I finally convince them that we're not ready to introduce these products, but, sometimes, I think the marketing people believe that actuaries are too cautious.

4:00 p.m. I discuss the meeting with some of the other actuaries on staff. We all know that poorly planned policies have spelled disaster for companies, and we agree that a lot more groundwork is needed to make sure that our new policies are ready for buyers and will look good to them. Otherwise, the products won't sell. We also need to be sure that our new policies will be profitable for the company.

Thanks to actuaries, insurance agents are able to offer people good insurance coverage at reasonable prices, while still making profits for their companies.

This twenty-story building in Des Moines, Iowa, is the home office of EMC Insurance Companies. EMC helps support one of the few true actuarial science programs in the United States, offered at Drake University.

Bank Manager

What is a bank manager?

Bank managers are responsible for the daily operations of banks and the delivery of banking services to the public. A bank manager may be in charge of a single, main banking office or one or more smaller branches of a particular bank. A large bank will often employ a manager for each specialized department, such as deposit accounts, which include checking and savings services; loan accounts, including mortgages on homes; and special services, such as **e-banking**.

Today, many banks have Web sites that allow customers to view their account information and even carry out bank transactions over the Internet.

Banks offer face-to-face service to customers who want to come inside the bank and transact their business personally. In addition, telephone, postal, and online banking services allow customers to carry out transactions twenty-four hours a day.

Fifty years ago, customers who wanted to withdraw money from their accounts had to visit their banks during fairly limited hours of operation. Today, most bank customers have cards, called debit cards or check

Vatican City Bank

Vatican City, which is the center of government for the Roman Catholic Church, is the smallest country in the world. Located in Rome, the capital of Italy, this country within a country has a population of only about nine hundred. Despite its small size, Vatican City has its own currency, postage stamps, and national bank.

While some customers still prefer face-to-face banking, the use of ATMs has increased rapidly in recent years.

cashing cards, that can be used to withdraw money, whenever they wish, from cash dispensing machines known as ATMs. Most banks have on-site ATMs for use by customers after normal banking hours. ATMs are also available in supermarkets, shopping malls, and many other locations. The wide use of computerized banking systems, these days, means that fewer people work in banks, but it also means that bank staff can give walk-in customers more time and attention.

A bank manager's overall responsibilities are to make sure that the daily functions of the bank are carried out smoothly, that staff are performing their jobs well, and that customers are receiving good service. More specific responsibilities fall into several different areas:

Business
- promoting the bank to increase the number of customers
- selling bank products, including checking accounts, mortgage and **consumer loans**, savings and other **investment** accounts, and credit cards

Bank employees are trained to be courteous, efficient, and accurate in their dealings with customers.

Staff management
- hiring and training staff
- motivating staff to work hard
- determining and enforcing policies and procedures
- dealing with employee performance problems and providing reviews, or evaluations, on a regular basis

Good Points and Bad Points

"As a bank manager in a small town, I've gotten to know many of our customers well, and I enjoy giving them personalized service."

"Banking jobs are more demanding than they used to be. These days, bank managers are expected to increase business, so I always have to be thinking about how to attract new customers, as well as how to keep our current customers."

- organizing work and vacation schedules to ensure having enough staff during all hours of operation

Customer service
- educating customers on banking services and how best to use them
- taking care of business for customers with complex transactions or special cases that cannot be handled through standard operating procedures
- assisting customers with special problems, such as transaction errors or overdue loan payments
- dealing with customer complaints
- determining customer needs and developing new products and services to meet those needs

Bank administration
Bank managers are responsible for banking systems, the safety of the staff, and security of the building and its contents. Although managers may not do all of these jobs themselves, they are in charge of appointing others to do them and making sure the work is done properly. A bank's administrative jobs include:

A manager who works for a large, international bank, such as the Hong Kong and Shanghai Banking Corporation (HSBC), needs education and experience that is equal to the job's complex responsibilities.

- monitoring computer and other electronic systems
- managing control procedures, such as error tracking, daily and monthly transaction balancing, internal audits, and **fraud** prevention
- making sure that the building, cash, and all other valuable or confidential materials are secure

Main qualifications of a bank manager

Interpersonal skills

Bank managers need to enjoy working with, helping, and supervising people and must know how to be courteous and friendly, even in difficult situations. As supervisors, they must be patient and considerate but still make sure employees perform well. When dealing with upset or angry customers, they must stay calm and try to be as helpful as possible, even when they have to be firm in applying policies and procedures.

Flexibility

Banking as an industry is part of the world's constantly changing economic and financial environment, and anyone working in the industry must be able to adapt to frequent changes in what they do, how they do it, and even who they work for.

Knowing their products and communicating their expertise effectively helps bank managers win the trust and confidence of their customers.

Mathematical ability

Most bank transactions involve working with numbers and mathematical calculations. Although very advanced mathematics skills are not usually required, bank managers must be accurate and confident in their use of math.

Communication skills

While written communication skills are important for preparing letters, product information, and other documents, verbal skills may be even more important for bank managers. They must be able to communicate clear, complete instructions to staff, as well as straightforward, understandable information to customers.

Bank managers must make sure that all systems in the bank run smoothly and remain secure. Their duties can include anything from answering customers' questions to opening and closing the vault.

Computer skills

Today, all banking systems are computerized. Bank managers must know how to use these systems, detect problems, and make sure the systems operate efficiently.

Knowledge of banking products and procedures

Banks offer customers many different financial services and many different kinds of savings, investment, and loan products. Bank managers must have a good understanding of and aptitude for the banking business and be able to not only keep pace with changes and developments but also explain them to staff members and sell them to customers.

fact file

Bank management jobs do not necessarily require any special education or training, but course work in accounting, finance, or banking can be helpful. Often, bank employees are promoted to managers after either taking classes, such as those offered by the American Bankers Association, or proving their professional and technical excellence on the job.

Leon Jamison

Leon joined his bank as a management trainee seven years ago, after completing a two-year associate degree program in banking and financial support services. He now manages two branch offices.

8:30 a.m. I arrive at one of the branch banks I manage. I usually spend two days a week at one branch and two days at the other, with one day at the main office. The schedule can vary from week to week.

9:15 a.m. A new employee arrives. I welcome her, show her around, introduce her to the staff, and contact the main office to schedule training. Until she completes her formal training program, she will work alongside one of our experienced staff members, mainly observing transactions.

10:00 a.m. I interview a customer who is applying for a loan. He is a farmer and wants to borrow money to build a new cattle barn. The loan he wants is large, but he has been a customer for many years. He is also a good businessman and has brought along a business plan for me to review.

11:45 a.m. We have gone over the business plan, but it needs to be revised, and I have to ask the customer to reduce the amount of money he wants to borrow. I arrange to meet with the customer, again, next week. If everything is in order by then, we can go ahead with processing his loan application.

12:00 p.m. I telephone the other branch office. While I was with the loan customer, a staff member called to report a few problems that need my attention.

1:00 p.m.   I have lunch with a possible new customer who is looking for a bank to handle his business accounts.

3:00 p.m.   I meet with a local business group that sponsors a college scholarship. My bank is **trustee** on the account that funds the scholarship. We discuss the distribution of money for this year's award.

5:00 p.m.   The staff are balancing their transactions for the day. I need to check and sign off on each cash drawer and return the drawers to the main vault.

6:00 p.m.   Everything is secure, so I can lock up and go home.

Although well-trained bank employees are able to take care of most banking transactions, managers are often called upon to handle complicated situations or problems.

Bank managers spend a lot of time with some customers. The details of certain transactions, such as mortgage loans or IRAs, require careful explanation.

Economist

What is an economist?

Economists study the ways in which societies use the resources they possess to produce goods and services. These resources include labor, **capital**, machinery, and equipment, as well as land and raw materials such as petroleum, iron, coal, and other minerals.

Economics comes from a Greek word meaning "house-hold management." In the modern use of the term, economics is about deciding what to produce, how to produce it, and for whom, especially making choices in the face of **scarcity**.

Dr. R. K. Pachauri is an economist, an industrial engineer, and the head of an energy research institute. His study of climate change has provided the United Nations Environment Network with valuable social and economic information.

Economists gather and analyze information to help governments, businesses, and institutions develop successful economic programs and strategies, and to recommend ways to meet the economic challenges of the future.

The study of economics has two main branches:

- microeconomics looks at details of the economy, focusing both on particular **markets** for products and services and on how buyers and sellers interact
- macroeconomics is a broad view of the economy that looks at financial systems and cycles

Adam Smith

Economist and philosopher Adam Smith was born in Scotland in 1723. In his famous book, *The Wealth of Nations*, written in 1776, Smith developed the idea of a **free market**. His theory argued that private enterprise, rather than government control, was the most efficient way to use a nation's resources. Today, many economists still support Smith's theory.

A country's economy goes through cycles of ups and downs. The "ups" are periods of growth, called expansion; the "downs" are called recessions. Both expansions and recessions can bring problems. Economists track what the economy is doing, trying to foresee problems and possibly prevent them or at least keep them under control.

Coal is one of many natural resources that can produce wealth for a country.

During periods of rapid expansion, inflation is a problem that gets a lot of attention. Inflation is a general rise in prices or a decline in the purchasing power of money. During periods of recession, one of the main problems is usually unemployment. Some economists say that the best economy is a "goldilocks" economy — not too hot (fast), not too cold (slow), but just right.

Main responsibilities of an economist

The variety of work done by economists falls into three main areas of responsibility.

- Research — To obtain the information they need for analysis and decision making, economists track economic trends and gather data in a variety of ways. They might, for example, use different sampling techniques to gain information through surveys.

- Assessment — Economists examine information and data and analyze them to determine their effects on the economic systems, situations, or problems they are studying or to develop forecasts of future economic trends. They also develop and test theories of how markets and economies function.

- Presentation — Economists write reports, and prepare tables and charts to present the results of their research and analysis to clients, employers, or the general public. As a rule, presentations also include recommendations for some kind of action to resolve or avoid problems or to take advantage of opportunities.

In 1992, U. S. economist Gary Becker, who is a professor of economics at the University of Chicago, won the Nobel Prize for economics. Becker's recent research includes the economics of the family and the influence of social forces on the economy.

Good Points and Bad Points

"I like that my job is varied and interesting and deals with a lot of practical research."

"When I say I'm an economist, people tend to think that I'm some sort of dusty professor who thinks up weird ideas."

Economists work for a wide range of organizations, either as company employees or as hired consultants.

Corporations and industries employ economists to:

- determine the demand for their products and services and to forecast sales
- analyze the growth of competitors and give advice on how to handle competition
- monitor changes in laws and regulations and assess their impact on particular industries
- give advice on how to invest their **assets** and grow their businesses

Financial institutions, such as banks, insurance companies, and **investment** firms, employ economists to:

- keep track of national and international economic trends that affect loans and investments
- forecast changes in inflation, unemployment, **interest** rates, and other economic indicators
- monitor changes in laws and regulations
- give advice on investments to produce growth

Governments employ economists to:

- collect economic data
- monitor national and international economies
- assess the economic effects of laws and policies
- suggest steps to deal with economic problems

Economists advise both businesses and governments on how to plan economic and financial strategies. U. S. president George W. Bush often meets with senior business representatives to discuss current economic issues.

Main qualifications of an economist

Knowledge of economics

A good background in both macroeconomics and microeconomics is needed to work in any economic specialty. All economists also need to know about economic theories, including their history, development, and how they affect world economies today.

Strong mathematics background

Numbers and calculations are part of every economist's job, so knowledge of math and statistics is essential. All economists need to have quantitative skills, which means they have to be able to express and measure information in quantities or amounts.

Many economists teach in colleges and universities. Work schedules in an academic environment are often flexible enough to allow time for research or consulting activities as well as teaching.

Research experience

Economists spend a lot of time examining information and considering its effect on present conditions and how it might influence future developments. Experience in gathering information and data and in conducting interviews and surveys is especially important for starting a career as an economist. In the beginning, the focus of an economist's work is often research.

Analytical ability

Many of an economist's responsibilities involve precise data analysis.

Alan Greenspan has been a chief economist for the United States government since the 1970s and is currently serving his fifth four-year term as chairman of the **Federal Reserve** Board.

Economists need to pick out important points from huge amounts of information, figure out what they mean, and judge how significant they might be.

Communication skills

After collecting and analyzing information, economists must deliver their findings and recommendations to others. Whether communicating verbally or in writing, an economist must be clear, correct, concise, and easy to understand.

Computer skills

Economists use computers to find information and data, perform calculations, write reports, prepare statistical charts and graphs, and contact other economists throughout the world.

Patience and perseverance

Long hours of study and problem-solving are part of an economist's job, and there are no single correct answers.

fact file

Beginning jobs for economists require only a bachelor's degree in economics or a closely-related field, but the more responsible research jobs and administrative and teaching positions require a master's or doctoral degree. An **internship** in a research or consulting firm or a government agency is good work experience.

A day in the life of an economist

Sam Lane

Sam works as an economist for a government agency. He has a doctoral degree in economics and spent several years doing research at a university before taking his present job. He is currently working on a project to determine the amount of money that will be needed to fund education in the future.

8:30 a.m.   I attend a meeting to gather information from colleagues who have been looking at education policies in different countries.

10:00 a.m.   I continue my independent research work, examining data on possible future housing costs and trying to calculate how much prices are likely to go up. Housing is becoming very expensive, which usually means that the age at which couples buy a first home and start families will increase. When housing prices are high, couples also tend to buy smaller houses and have fewer children than their parents did. But will this trend continue? Families could become bigger, or people might move into certain areas from different parts of the country or from abroad. I have to consider all of these and many other possibilities.

As the workers of the future, children are important to a country's wealth. Quality education programs are vital if children are to play productive roles in a country's economy.

2:00 p.m.   My supervisor stops by to review my progress. One of her responsibilities is making sure my work stays on schedule. Because I work alone, it's easy to wander off track, following a line of research that, although interesting, is not necessarily central to the project. My supervisor specifies some issues she'd like me to focus on.

4:00 p.m.   I look over my notes from this morning's meeting to figure out how the information fits into the rest of my research.

5:30 p.m.   Before going home, I check my schedule and review what I want to accomplish tomorrow. In my line of work, planning ahead is essential.

Economics is closely linked with politics, and economists often become politicians. Alejandro Toledo, who was elected president of Peru in 2001, was an economics professor and has published many works on economic growth and reform.

Insurance Broker

What is an insurance broker?

Insurance **brokers** help individuals and businesses find and purchase insurance policies to protect their lives, health, and property against financial losses due to unforeseen events. Some people sell insurance as captive agents, which means they deal with products from only one company. Insurance brokers work independently, selling products from many companies.

Many people rely on insurance brokers to help them figure out what kinds of insurance they need, as well as how much they need.

The most common types of insurance products include:

- Life insurance — People insure their lives so that, when they die, anyone who depended on them for financial support will have some type of income.
- Homeowner's insurance — People who own homes insure their buildings and possessions so that when fires, floods, burglaries, or other events damage or destroy their property, it can be replaced.

Lloyd's of London

In 1688, shipowners and merchants, wanting to avoid financial disasters when ships were lost at sea, met at Edward Lloyd's coffeehouse in London, England, and made insurance deals with each other to protect their ships and cargo. These agreements were the start of the famous Lloyd's of London, which, today, is the oldest continuously operating insurance business in the world.

- Auto insurance — People buy insurance to protect themselves financially against loss or damage to their cars, trucks, or other motor vehicles due to theft, accidents, or vandalism. Besides insuring the repair or replacement of their own vehicles, drivers are also insured to be able to pay financial **compensation** if they damage another vehicle or injure a person with a motor vehicle.

- Health insurance — People insure their health to help pay the high costs of medical care for treating and preventing illnesses.

- Business insurance — Companies carry insurance to protect their businesses from losses due to property damage, accidents, crime, and other harmful events.

The main floor of the Lloyd's building in London, England, is crowded with insurance brokers. Since 1984, this modern, high-tech building on Lime Street has been the headquarters for Lloyd's of London.

Main responsibilities of an insurance broker

Helping people make good decisions about their insurance needs and the best products to purchase usually involves:

- discussing what a client has to protect and what the client expects from an insurance policy
- determining how much the client can afford to pay for insurance
- doing research to find different policies that meet the client's particular needs
- advising the client on the best policy for the price
- guiding the client through the paperwork and other procedures required to purchase a policy

Many brokers also assist clients in filing **claims** for losses that are covered by their insurance policies, and all

Brokers sometimes need to visit the sites of buildings that people want to insure. Before certain policies can be written, a broker has to assess the **risks** of the property.

Good Points and Bad Points

"Clients usually rely on me to do their research, and I enjoy finding the best insurance policies for them."

"Sometimes, the work is extremely complicated, especially when I need to find insurers that will cover a big project of some kind. Being an insurance broker for large institutions and corporations is important for business, but it can be very difficult and time consuming."

brokers make themselves available to answer clients' questions about either particular policies or insurance in general.

When a risk that a client wants to insure is very large or very expensive, such as an aircraft, a broker's job can become quite complex. The insurance often has to be spread among several different companies, so the broker has to, first, find companies that are able to share the risk and, then, negotiate and coordinate the terms of insurance with each of the companies.

Some insurance brokers specialize in a single type of insurance, such as marine insurance, which protects boats and other watercraft.

Main qualifications of an insurance broker

Knowledge of mathematics, business, and finance

Insurance calculations can be complicated, so brokers must be able to work quickly and confidently with numbers, and most insurance companies prefer that brokers have some kind of background in business, finance, or economics. Brokers must also keep up with developments in the financial world, including tax laws and federal and state insurance regulations.

Integrity

Insurance brokers make their money from **commissions** they receive by selling policies, but they must always put their clients' interests first, recommending the best policies, not the ones that pay the highest commissions.

Brokers and executives from national and international insurance companies meet at conferences and conventions to review and discuss products and services, as well as laws and regulations that affect insurers.

Brokers must earn and keep the trust and confidence of their customers. Keeping clients satisfied is also necessary to gain new business through referrals.

The widespread use of computers throughout the insurance industry has helped brokers serve their clients faster and more efficiently.

Sales skills

A broker's success depends on selling insurance products, so brokers must always be looking for new clients. Finding clients is hard work that requires determination and enthusiasm, as well as expert knowledge of the insurance industry.

fact file

A college degree in business or economics or proven sales ability are two possible ways to start a career as an insurance broker. Selling insurance, however, always requires one or more state licenses, earned by passing appropriate examinations.

Communication skills

Whether they are selling policies, negotiating claims, or giving financial presentations, insurance brokers do a lot of talking. They also have to write reports and maintain records. All of these tasks require clear, careful communication, and close attention to details.

Computer skills

With the growth of technology, especially the Internet, computers are now used widely in the insurance industry for research, presenting products, calculating costs, comparing policies, keeping records, and more.

A day in the life of an insurance broker

Suzanne Gray

Suzanne started selling insurance as a captive agent for an insurance company. She later started her own business as an insurance broker, finding products to suit her clients through many different companies.

9:00 a.m. I'm driving to a client's home. Since buying his house, he has started to run a business there, restoring classic cars in some of the outbuildings on the property. We're going to discuss changes to his homeowner's policy as well as **liability** insurance for his business. He also wants to look into workers' compensation insurance for the staff he is hoping to employ, so he will have financial protection if an employee is injured at work.

10:00 a.m. Throughout our discussion, I make notes on what my client wants. A home business is a complicated matter, and the costs of different coverages add up quickly. I try to suggest ways to help keep costs down, such as pointing out that installing burglar alarms could reduce the cost of theft coverage.

12:30 p.m. On the way back to my office, I stop for lunch and review my notes from the meeting.

2:00 p.m. Back at my desk, I check my E-mail and phone messages and discover that there may be a problem at one of the insurance companies I deal with. I make a few phone calls, trying to find out if a rumor that the company might be taken over is accurate. No luck, for now, but I'll make more inquiries later. Meanwhile, I'll be cautious about selling policies from that company.

3:00 p.m. I return a phone call from a possible new client who's planning to start an animal grooming business. A friend of hers recommended me. I arrange to meet with her in a couple of days.

3:30 p.m. I take another look at my notes from this morning and start researching appropriate products for my client. I want to have information for him within a week. I don't like to keep clients waiting too long.

5:30 p.m. I have a good start on some policies for my client but will have to wait, now, until morning to contact companies to negotiate pricing.

Hurricane victims in Florida lined up outside an insurance office, waiting to file property damage claims.

Finding the right policies for clients can take a lot of research, and brokers need to be sure that their calculations are accurate.

Investment Banker

What is an investment banker?

Investment bankers are advisors or **intermediaries** who help companies make business deals. Investment banks assist clients in borrowing money, selling **shares** to investors, buying or selling companies, or carrying out any business transactions that require complicated analysis and negotiation. **Compensation** for services is a fee between 1 and 10 percent of the value of the deal negotiated. By contrast, a **commercial bank** lends money, offers savings and checking accounts, and makes its **revenue** mainly from **interest** on loans.

For about fifty of its more than 135-year history, Goldman Sachs has had its head-quarters on Broad Street in New York City. The firm constructed its own towering office building at 85 Broad Street in 1983.

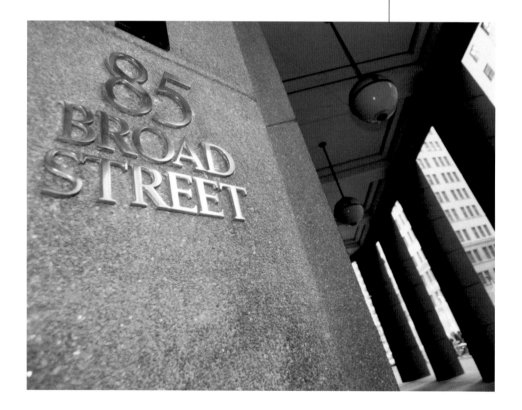

Goldman Sachs

Goldman Sachs is one of the world's leading and most profitable investment banks. The firm was founded in 1869 and entered the field of investment banking in 1906. Goldman Sachs operates throughout the world, especially in leading financial centers such as New York, Frankfurt, London, and Hong Kong.

Investment banking can be a very **profitable** business. If, for example, an investment bank helps a client buy a company for one hundred million dollars, even a 2 percent fee, or two million dollars, is a nice reward. The team of bankers who worked on the deal is often awarded a bonus of up to half of the fee.

Making deals requires a lot of communication among bankers, clients, lawyers, and accountants. Each group plays an important role in a business deal.

There is a **risk**, however, in this profession. For most of their services, investment bankers are paid only if a deal is completed. Their fee is called a "success fee." If a deal is not completed, there is no success and no fee. Sometimes, bankers work hard on a deal for weeks or months, but do not complete it, and no fee is paid.

Main responsibilities of an investment banker

The services investment bankers offer clients include:

Business development
Bankers who are experts in a client's industry will:

- study the company's products and services as well as the **market**, customers, and competitors

The global reach of their profession means investment bankers may have to spend a lot of time traveling. Investment banks are involved in financial dealings all over the world.

Good Points and Bad Points

"I love the fast-paced environment of investment banking and the opportunity it gives me to work with so many intelligent people. We never stop learning from each other."

"The long work hours are stressful, especially in the weeks before a critical deadline. The job is rewarding in many ways, but it leaves me with very little free time."

- use the information they gather to create plans to make the company stronger and more valuable
- present plans to clients to get corporate finance, **underwriting**, and **mergers** and **acquisitions** (M&A) assignments

Corporate finance

Plans for growth often call for more money than a company has on hand. A corporate finance banker will:

- analyze the situation and help the company decide how much money it needs, whether to borrow or seek investors, and which lenders and investors to approach
- work with the company to negotiate with lenders and investors

Public securities

The larger investment banks are licensed to sell **securities** to the public, which means they can place shares of a company on a **stock exchange**. An investment banker deals with the client, working closely with a **broker**, who sells the client's shares to institutions and individuals.

Mergers and Acquisitions

An M&A investment banker acts as an advisor to clients in buying or selling companies. The banker helps a client determine what to buy or sell and at what price. The banker also helps negotiate the deal.

Main qualifications of an investment banker

Interpersonal skills
In investment banking, relationships are formed between companies and banks, but what makes them work are relationships among people. Investment bankers must be capable of making and keeping strong, trusting relationships with both clients and the many other professionals who work with them on transactions.

Integrity and professionalism
Clients pay investment banks very well for services so they expect investment bankers to be attentive and trustworthy. In investment banking, as in every profession, keeping promises, doing things on time, and being truthful in all dealings with others are essential to retaining clients and maintaining good relationships with coworkers.

Investment bankers are paid well, but most of them work long hours. Some report working seventy to one hundred hours a week.

Communication skills
Written and verbal communication are tools used daily by investment bankers. They speak with others to gather and share information and frequently write proposals and reports to clients and coworkers. Writing skills are particularly important because a lot of an investment banker's persuading and selling must be done in written form.

The European Union (EU) has its own investment bank that provides services to EU member countries and to other governments. In 2000, Francis Mayer (left), who, then, was vice president of the European Investment Bank, helped the Syrian government borrow money to modernize its electricity network.

Business and finance experience

Knowledge of business and finance is a good foundation for a job in investment banking, but proven success in the use of knowledge and skills is important, too. Investment banks and their clients prefer to work with bankers who have real-life experience.

fact file

A bachelor's degree in almost any field is enough to qualify for a job in an investment bank, but these banks hire only candidates who have outstanding academic records, and degrees in business-related fields, economics, law, or mathematics are preferred.

Computer and math skills

Knowing how to use computers for research, analysis, and communication is essential for today's investment bankers, who are constantly gathering, organizing, analyzing, and sharing information with others. Projects often involve complicated financial analysis, which requires basic math skills and mastery of financial software, such as spreadsheet programs.

A day in the life of an investment banker

Claire Regan

Claire started working in an investment bank seven years ago, right after she graduated with a degree in statistics. The focus of her job is bringing new clients to the bank.

8:15 a.m.   We're pitching for a new client this morning, which means that a company is looking for an investment bank, and we are competing with several other banks for the account. I'm part of a small group that will give a presentation to the company to try to convince them that we are the right investment bank to meet their needs. I've been up since 6:00 a.m., thinking about the kinds of questions we might be asked.

10:00 a.m.   The presentation has started. Although we're all a little tense, we are also confident that our organization is a strong competitor.

12:00 p.m.   A feedback session after the presentation reassures me that everything went well and, after answering all of the prospective client's questions, I'm free to grab a sandwich and coffee for lunch.

12:45 p.m.   Back at my desk, I check my E-mails and find an urgent message. One of our clients, a large chemical manufacturing company, is considering the acquisition, or takeover, of a competing company that makes soaps and toiletries. The client wants to meet with us this afternoon. I contact the company immediately.

1:00 p.m.   I try to convince the client that I need some time to do research and calculations before I will be able to give any guidance on the advisability of a takeover or the best way to proceed. After a long phone conversation, we arrange to meet the day after tomorrow.

4:00 p.m. I check my in-box for documents that I have to examine and pass on to clients. I tackle as many as I can before making some phone calls about the manufacturing client's proposed business deal.

6:30 p.m. I meet with colleagues for dinner. I need to pick their brains on several client-related matters.

Early in his career, Hungarian-born billionaire George Soros worked briefly as a trainee in a London investment bank. Soros made his fortune, however, as a **fund manager**.

This Citibank office is in Seoul, South Korea. In 2004, Citigroup, a global investment bank, took control of KorAm Bank, marking the largest-ever foreign investment in South Korea.

Stockbroker

What is a stockbroker?

Stockbrokers coordinate the buying and selling of **securities** for investors. When a company needs to raise money, it issues **shares** of stock that can be purchased at a set price per share. By purchasing shares, an investor gains a small portion of ownership in the company. The more shares an investor buys, the greater his or her portion of ownership.

People who buy stock are called shareholders because, by owning even small parts of the companies in which they invest money, they share in the profits and losses.

Securities are typically traded through a **stock exchange**. Many stockbrokers, however, work for companies through which investors buy and sell shares online or by phone. This method of investing is known as over-the-counter (OTC) trading.

The reason shareholders buy stock is to make money. Their goal is to purchase shares when they are low in price and sell them when the shares are worth higher prices, making a **profit** on their **investments**.

The Buttonwood Agreement

In 1792, twenty-four of New York's top investment **brokers** tried to bring order to the city's **haphazard** securities business. Gathered at their usual meeting place, under a buttonwood tree on Wall Street, they agreed to trade securities for a set **commission** and only among themselves, instead of through trade auctions conducted in parks and coffeehouses. This pact laid the foundation for the New York Stock Exchange.

This illustration shows the outside of the New York Stock Exchange building as it looked in the 1800s.

VIEW OF THE STOCK EXCHANGE AND BROAD STREET.

Stockbrokers help people make investments. They read reports written by financial analysts and monitor daily activities in investment **markets**, then use what they learn to advise their clients on what securities to buy and when to buy or sell shares. They also make sure that clients' transactions are carried out.

Stockbrokers' clients include individuals, corporations and companies, **pension** funds, financial institutions, and nonprofit organizations. Brokers stay in close contact with their clients, recommending certain investments, discouraging others, and giving reasons for their advice.

Main responsibilities of a stockbroker

Handling another person's or an organization's money is a huge responsibility. Stockbrokers' specific tasks, however, depend on the level of service they offer.

- Full-service stockbrokers help clients figure out investment strategies and advise them on which securities to purchase. They develop **portfolios** for clients and review the portfolios on a regular basis to make sure that the investments are doing well and continuing to meet clients' needs. In return, they are paid a fee (usually a percentage of the **assets** managed) or a commission (usually a percentage of a particular transaction).

- Discount stockbrokers carry out orders from investors to buy and sell securities but give little, if any, advice and receive a comparatively low fee for each transaction.

A telephone is an essential tool for a stockbroker, for both contacting clients and taking care of their stock transactions.

Good Points and Bad Points

"I like excitement, and I like being kept on my toes. Working with the ups and downs of the market and being responsible for other people's money is the perfect job for me."

"The atmosphere in the stock exchange is noisy and hectic. I love this kind of work environment, but stressful conditions like these don't suit everyone."

Stockbrokers at work monitor the continually changing prices of securities and fluctuations in world money markets on quote boards and computer terminals. To help clients take advantage of investment opportunities, transactions must often be made very quickly.

Most stockbrokers serve individual investors. An investor pays a stockbroker a commission on each transaction, expecting to benefit from the broker's financial knowledge and expertise. In this kind of business relationship, fairness and honesty are a stockbroker's most fundamental responsibilities and include:

- loyalty to customers and always putting the interests of investors first
- doing careful research to fully understand any investment presented to a client for consideration
- providing clients with all the information they need to select investments that best suit their needs
- knowing a client's financial status, investment objectives, level of understanding, and tolerance for **risk** and recommending only investments that are appropriate for the client's financial situation

Main qualifications of a stockbroker

Knowledge of financial markets

Stockbrokers must fully understand economic principles, securities of all kinds, and how investment activities in any part of the world affect markets all over the world.

Mathematics and computer skills

The world of investments is a world of numbers and calculations. Stockbrokers must be competent with figures, percentages, projections, and many other mathematical functions. Because the securities business is so highly automated, computer skills are also essential and must be kept up to date.

The arrow on this display for the Hang Seng Index indicates that the closing prices of shares traded on the Hong Kong stock exchange ended down more than 574 points for the day.

Sales experience

A big part of a stockbroker's job is finding new clients, so having sales skills can be very important. In selling their services, stockbrokers have to keep in mind that being pleasant is as important as being persuasive. Most people will not take financial advice from a person they do not like or trust.

Confidence

Stockbrokers work under a lot of pressure and are often expected to process information and act on it very quickly. This kind of work requires a high level of self-confidence and the ability to work independently.

These days, the business of trading securities is extremely automated. Stockbrokers have to keep their computer skills up to date and be able to use many kinds of electronic equipment.

fact file

Jobs for stockbrokers usually require a college education. Although a stockbroker's degree can be in almost any academic field, courses in business administration, finance, economics, marketing, and law are very helpful and may be required. Some positions may also require a master's degree, such as an M.B.A. (Master of Business Administration), and ongoing training is essential to keep up with changing laws and regulations, as well as new financial products. Stockbrokers must be licensed and registered securities agents, which requires employment in a registered firm for at least four months and passing a series of exams.

Communication skills

To most people, investments are complicated financial matters. Investors depend on professionals such as stockbrokers to provide clear explanations and advice. To win the trust of their clients, stockbrokers must also have good interpersonal skills.

Integrity

Because stockbrokers often deal with huge amounts of money on behalf of clients, their business practices and financial transactions are subject to many laws and a strict code of conduct that is monitored by government and other regulatory agencies and by professional associations.

A day in the life of a stockbroker

Damien Dean

Damien has a degree in business management. He is currently working as a stockbroker in the investments area of a large **commercial bank**.

5:30 a.m.   I'm up early, as usual, so I can catch news of the opening markets.

8:00 a.m.   As soon as I arrive at the office, I attend a brief morning meeting at which the staff reviews a roundup of global financial news. In today's financial world, there's always something going on somewhere throughout the night.

8:45 a.m.   Even during coffee breaks, my conversations with colleagues are almost always about work.

9:00 a.m.   Frequently throughout the day, I read newspapers and financial journals and check news and financial Internet sites. I need to keep up with current events because of their effects on financial markets. Unrest in oil-producing countries, for example, is usually bad news, and elections that bring changes in government also need to be watched.

9:15 a.m.   I spend some time looking for new clients and making telephone calls to introduce myself to potential customers. When I hear rumors about companies and institutions that are not happy with their brokerage firms, I'm on the phone to those organizations right away.

12:00 p.m. I attend a business lunch with a prospective client. I've spoken with this person a number of times by phone, but a face-to-face meeting and buying a prospective client lunch often helps close the deal.

1:30 p.m. I take phone calls from clients who want to buy or sell investments. Some of them know exactly what they want — they just need me to handle the transaction; but most want advice, too.

4:00 p.m. I review clients' portfolios to see how their investments are doing and to determine whether I can suggest anything to help them make more money.

5:30 p.m. I leave the office with enough time to eat dinner before going to a local community college, where I'm teaching a six-week investment class.

This New York stockbroker often spends his evenings helping students from a local high school learn business mathematics.

Stockbrokers in Tokyo watched with dismay as stock prices fell sharply in August 1990.

Glossary

acquisition – the process of gaining control, or taking over, a company or corporation, usually by purchasing or exchanging stock

alloy – a metal such as brass or bronze, which is made by combining two or more pure metals or metallic elements

annuities – insurance contracts that provide owners with payments, made at specific intervals, which are usually used as income during retirement

asset – an amount of cash or an item or object that has value, especially property, securities, or other investments that can be sold for or converted to cash

audit – (v) to examine and confirm or correct the accuracy of a company's financial records and accounts

bartered – traded or exchanged goods or services without using money

brokers – people whose business is selling financial products or services from which they earn commissions

capital – money, property, and other assets, or their cash values, which can be used or invested to make more money

caravan – a group of vehicles or animals carrying goods from one place to another, usually over a long distance

claim – a request for payment based on the terms of an insurance policy

commercial bank – a financial institution that takes deposits, makes loans, and provides other money- and investment-related services to the general public

commissions – the fees paid to brokers for their assistance with investment transactions, such as buying or selling securities or real estate

compensation – an amount of money or property given in exchange for labor or other services or to replace something of value that has been lost, damaged, or destroyed

comply – to meet the terms of laws, regulations, requirements, or requests

consumer loans – amounts of money provided by lenders to borrowers for purchasing goods or services that are not usually backed by assets

e-banking – making bank deposits, loan payments, or other financial transactions online over the Internet

ethically – according to acceptable or moral standards and practices

expenditures – assets used up or paid out (spent) in exchange for goods or services

Federal Reserve – a system of banks established by the U. S. Congress to control the flow and value of money in the United States, to oversee banks throughout the country, and to help maintain a strong and stable economy

fraud – the act of intentionally misleading or deceiving, usually for financial gain

free market – an economic system that allows supply and demand, rather than government policies, to regulate prices and wages

fund manager – the person who makes financial decisions about the securities in an investment fund to make sure the fund meets its stated goals

haphazard – without order or direction

interest – compensation paid to a lender for the use of borrowed money or capital

intermediaries – the people who take a middle position between buyers and sellers in business deals and try to keep transactions on track and moving forward

internship – a period of training or practice to learn a profession on the job

investment – the use of cash or other capital to create financial gain, such as putting money into a business with the intention of earning a share of the business's profits

IRA – short for "individual retirement account," in which investments made to provide retirement income can increase in value without being taxed until the funds are withdrawn

liability – having to do with financial expense, debt, or possible loss

markets – public places where or through which people buy or sell goods or services or exchange money or property

merger – the process of combining two or more companies, either through acquisition or by pulling together their assets and resources

pension – having to do with payments and other benefits from an employer that are received after retirement

portfolio – a collection of securities and other investments that are owned by a single individual or organization

profits – the financial gains of businesses or investments after all expenses have been subtracted

renovates – repairs or restores

revenue – the amount of income received by a company or organization during a specific period of time

risks – objects or activities that carry the possibility for some kind of loss, especially financial loss

scarcity – the condition or state of lacking something or having only small quantities or supplies of something

securities – stocks, bonds, profit-sharing agreements, and most other investment products, except insurance

shares – the units of ownership in a company or a mutual fund

stock exchange – a financial market where shares of stock are bought and sold in compliance with strict rules and procedures

trustee – a person or organization entrusted with investing and managing an individual's or organization's assets

underwriting – the procedure through which new securities are offered for sale to the public. An underwriter guarantees to the company issuing the securities a set price for a certain number of shares so the issuer is ensured a minimum amount from the sales of those shares.

Further Information

This book does not cover all of the jobs in the banking and finance industries. Many jobs are not mentioned, including bank tellers, insurance underwriters, and financial advisors. This book does, however, give you an idea of what working in banking and finance is like.

The financial world is fast-paced, and anyone who wants to work in it needs to be able to cope with pressure and stress. Some jobs require more energy and commitment than others, but the emphasis is always on bringing in new business and making more money. For those who are successful, the rewards can be great. Many jobs offer opportunities to earn high salaries. For a person who is confident working with figures, enjoys a challenge, and has plenty of ambition, a job in banking or finance could be just right.

The only way to decide if working in banking or finance is right for you is to find out what jobs in these fields involve. Read as much as you can about financial careers and talk to people, especially people you know, who work in the banking or finance industry.

When you are in middle school or high school, a teacher or career counselor might be able to help you arrange to spend some time in a bank or an insurance office, or visit a stock exchange, so you can watch what goes on and how the people who work there spend their time.

Books

Career Ideas for kids who like Math
Diane Lindsey Reeves
(Facts on File, 2000)

Career Ideas for kids who like Money
Diane Lindsey Reeves and Gayle Bryan
(Facts on File, 2001)

Careers for the Twenty-First Century: Finance
Patrice Cassedy
(Lucent Books, 2003)

Choosing a Career in Banking and Finance
Carolyn Simpson
(Rosen, 1999)

Web Sites

Be An Actuary: A Career Without Boundaries
www.BeAnActuary.org

CareerKids.com: Bank Managers
www.careerkids.com/careers/bank_managers.html

Stockbroker – Buy Low, Sell High!
www.collegeview.com/career/careersearch/job_profiles/busfin/sb.html

Useful Addresses

Accountant

American Institute of Certified Public
  Accountants (AICPA)
1211 Avenue of the Americas
New York, NY 10036-8775
Tel: (212) 596-6200
www.aicpa.org/nolimits/index.htm

Institute of Management Accountants
10 Paragon Drive
Montvale, NJ 07645-1718
Tel: (201) 573-9000 (800) 638-4427
www.imanet.org

Actuary

American Academy of Actuaries
1100 17th Street NW, 7th floor
Washington, DC 20036
Tel: (202) 223-8196
www.actuary.org

Bank Manager

American Bankers Association
1120 Connecticut Avenue NW
Washington, DC 20036
Tel: (800) BANKERS (226-5377)
www.aba.com

Economist

American Economic Association
2014 Broadway, Suite 305
Nashville, TN 37203
Tel: (615) 322-2595
www.vanderbilt.edu/AEA/

National Association for
  Business Economics
1233 20th Street NW #505
Washington, DC 20036
Tel: (202) 463-6223
www.nabe.com

Insurance Broker

Independent Insurance Agents
  & Brokers of America
127 S. Peyton Street
Alexandria, VA 22314
Tel: (800) 221-7917
www.iiaa.org

Investment Banker

National Investment Banking Association
P. O. Box 6625
Athens, GA 30604
Tel: (706) 208-9620
www.nibanet.org

Stockbroker

National Association of Stockbrokers
5755 Oberlin Drive, Suite 311
San Diego, CA 92121
Tel: (858) 455-7422 (800) 222-8627
www.nastockbrokers.com

Securities Industry Association
120 Broadway, 35th floor
New York, NY 10271-0080
Tel: (212) 608-1500
www.sia.com

Index

DATE DUE			

DEMCO